ESSENTIAL ELEMENTS®
GUITAR ENSEMBLES

EARLY INTERMEDIATE

THE BEATLES

FOR THREE OR MO

CONTENTS

Arrangements by Mark Phillips

ISBN 978-1-4950-6910-9

HAL•LEONARD®

7777 W. BLUEMOUND RD. P.O. BOX 13819 MILWAUKEE, WI 53213

ALL YOU NEED IS LOVE

Words and Music by John Lennon and Paul McCartney

13
Am
C
G
Am
16
Dm
C
G
F
Em
Dm
Chorus
19
N.C.
C
D
G
22
C
D
G
C
E7
25
Am
C
F
G
1.
C
2.
C

BLACKBIRD

Words and Music by John Lennon and Paul McCartney

21
A7
D7sus4
G
2.
G
Bridge
F
Em
26
Dm
C
B♭6
1.
C
2.
A7
D7sus4
31
G
Am7
G/B
C
G/B
A7
D7sus4
D.S. al Coda
Coda
G
36
C
G/B
A7
D7sus4
1.
G
2.
G

ELEANOR RIGBY

Words and Music by John Lennon and Paul McCartney

14
C
18
Chorus
Em
Em7
Em6
C
To Coda
22
Em
Em7
Em6
C
2nd time, D.C. al Coda
(no repeat)
26
Em
Coda
C
Em

THE FOOL ON THE HILL

Words and Music by John Lennon and Paul McCartney

Chorus
17
Dm
B♭
Dm
B♭
21
C
Dm
To Coda
Interlude
25
D6
D6
⑤
⑥
sim.
29
Em/D
3
D6
3
33
Em7
3
D.S. al Coda
Coda
D6

GET BACK

Words and Music by John Lennon and Paul McCartney

Chorus
13
A7
D
16
A
G/A
D/A
A7
1.
19
D
A
2.
D
22
3.
D
A

HELTER SKELTER

Words and Music by John Lennon and Paul McCartney

16
20
C
24
D
A
Chorus
29
D
A
33
D
1.
A
Fine
2.
D.S. al Fine
(take 1st ending)

HERE COMES THE SUN

Words and Music by George Harrison

Chorus
16
D
G
E7
20
D
G
D/F♯
Em7
D
A
1.
D
let ring
let ring
let ring
let ring
24
A7
2.
D
G
D/F♯
Em7
let ring
let ring
let ring
27
D
A
F
C
G/B
G
D
let ring
let ring
let ring
let ring
let ring

IN MY LIFE

Words and Music by John Lennon and Paul McCartney

14
F
B♭
C
17
Am
D
Fm
1.
2.
20
C
G
24
Fm
N.C.
C
G
G7
C
rit.
rit.
let ring
rit.

LET IT BE

Words and Music by John Lennon and Paul McCartney

Verse
Moderately slow, in 2

Chorus
C Am G F
C G F C/E Dm7
1. 2.
Outro
C C F C G F
C F C G F C

LUCY IN THE SKY WITH DIAMONDS

Words and Music by John Lennon and Paul McCartney

22
C
F
B♭
28
C
G
Slower
D
Chorus
33
G
C
D
G
C
36
D
G
C
D
39
1.
2.
A

MICHELLE

Words and Music by John Lennon and Paul McCartney

17
Am
Am(maj7)
Am7
Am6
Fmaj7
21
E
D.S. al Coda
Coda
E
Am
Am(maj7)
Am7
Am6
25
Fmaj7
E
Outro
A
Dm7
29
G
D♯o7
E
D♯o7
32
1.
E
2.
E
A

NORWEGIAN WOOD

(This Bird Has Flown)

Words and Music by John Lennon and Paul McCartney

Bridge
17
Am
21
D
Am
26
Bm7
30
E
2nd time, D.C. al Coda
Coda
A

SOMETHING

Words and Music by George Harrison

To Coda 𝄌
1.
2.
19
F
E♭
G
E♭
G
A
Bridge
23
A
C♯m
F♯m
27
A
D
G
1.
A
31
2.
C
D.S. al Coda
𝄌 Coda
E♭
G/D
35
A
F
E♭
G/D
C

WHILE MY GUITAR GENTLY WEEPS

Words and Music by George Harrison

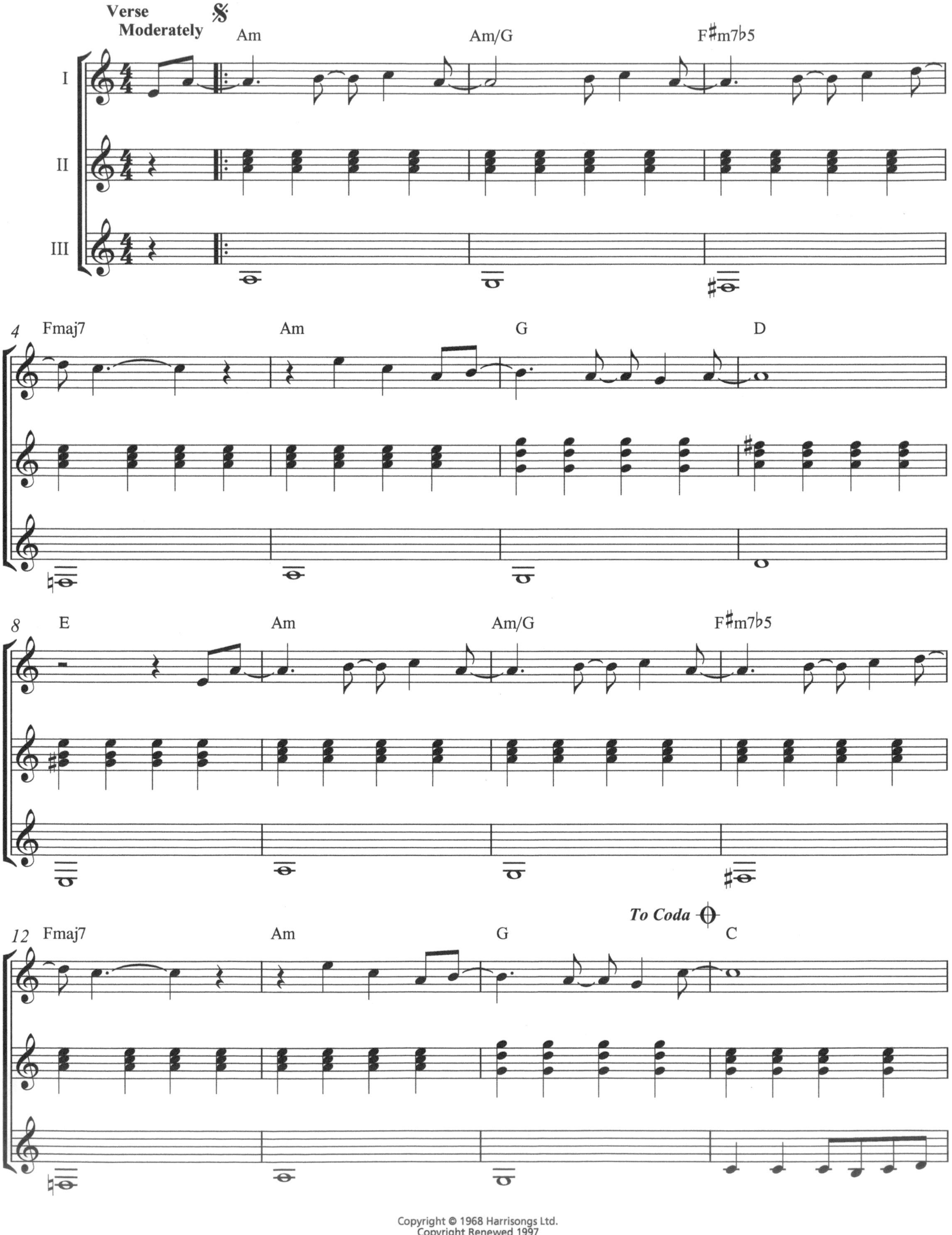

Bridge
16
E
A
C♯m
19
F♯m
C♯m
Bm
22
E
Dsus2/F♯
1.
E7/G♯
2.
E7/G♯
D.S. al Coda
25
Coda
C
E
Am

WITH A LITTLE HELP FROM MY FRIENDS

Words and Music by John Lennon and Paul McCartney

To Coda
1.
2.
Bridge
D.C. al Coda
Coda
C
G
D
Em7
A7
F
E♭
Cm6
13
16
19
22
25

ESSENTIAL ELEMENTS FOR GUITAR

Essential Elements Comprehensive Guitar Method

Take your guitar teaching to a new level! With popular songs in a variety of styles, and quality demonstration and backing tracks on the accompanying online audio, *Essential Elements for Guitar* is a staple of guitar teachers' instruction – and helps beginning guitar students off to a great start. This method was designed to meet the National Standards for Music Education, with features such as cross-curricular activities, quizzes, multicultural songs, basic improvisation and more.

BOOK 1

INCLUDES TAB

by Will Schmid and Bob Morris

Concepts covered in Book 1 include: getting started; basic music theory; guitar chords; notes on each string; music history; ensemble playing; performance spotlights; and much more! Songs include: Dust in the Wind • Eleanor Rigby • Every Breath You Take • Hey Jude • Hound Dog • Let It Be • Ode to Joy • Rock Around the Clock • Stand by Me • • Sweet Home Chicago • This Land Is Your Land • You Really Got Me • more!

00862639 Book/Online Audio..............$19.99
00001173 Book Only..........................$14.99

BOOK 2

by Bob Morris

Concepts taught in Book 2 include: playing melodically in positions up the neck; movable chord shapes up the neck; scales and extended chords in different keys; fingerpicking and pick style; improvisation in positions up the neck; and more! Songs include: Auld Lang Syne • Crazy Train • Folsom Prison Blues • La Bamba • Landslide • Nutcracker Suite • Sweet Home Alabama • Your Song • and more.

00865010 Book/Online Audio..............$22.99
00120873 Book Only..........................$14.99

Essential Elements Guitar Ensembles

The songs in the Essential Elements Guitar Ensemble series are playable by three or more guitars. Each arrangement features the melody, a harmony part, and bass line in standard notation along with chord symbols. For groups with more than three or four guitars, the parts can be doubled. This series is perfect for classroom guitar ensembles or other group guitar settings.

Mid-Beginner Level

EASY POP SONGS
00865011/$10.99

CHRISTMAS CLASSICS
00865015/$9.99

CHRISTMAS SONGS
00001136/$10.99

Late Beginner Level

CLASSICAL THEMES
00865005/$10.99

POP HITS
00001128/$12.99

ROCK CLASSICS
00865001/$10.99

Early Intermediate Level

J.S. BACH
00123103/$9.99

THE BEATLES
00172237/$12.99

CHRISTMAS FAVORITES
00128600/$12.99

DISNEY SONGS
00865014/$14.99

IRISH JIGS & REELS
00131525/$9.99

JAZZ BALLADS
00865002/$14.99

MULTICULTURAL SONGS
00160142/$9.99

POPULAR SONGS
00241053/$12.99

TOP SONGS 2010-2019
00295218/$9.99

Mid-Intermediate Level

THE BEATLES
00865008/$14.99

BOSSA NOVA
00865006/$12.99

CHRISTMAS CLASSICS
00865015/$9.99

DUKE ELLINGTON
00865009/$9.99

GREAT THEMES
00865012/$10.99

JIMI HENDRIX
00865013/$9.99

JAZZ STANDARDS
00865007/$14.99

ROCK HITS
00865017/$12.99

ROCK INSTRUMENTALS
00123102/$9.99

TOP HITS
00130606/$9.99

Late Intermediate to Advanced Level

JAZZ CLASSICS
00865016/$9.99

Essential Elements Guitar Songs

INCLUDES TAB

The books in the Essential Elements Guitar Songs series feature popular songs selected for the practice of specific guitar chord types. Each book includes eight songs and a CD with fantastic sounding play-along tracks. Practice at any tempo with the included Amazing Slow Downer software!

BARRE CHORD ROCK
00001137 Late-Beginner Level..........................$12.99

POWER CHORD ROCK
00001139 Mid-Beginner Level...........................$16.99

More Resources

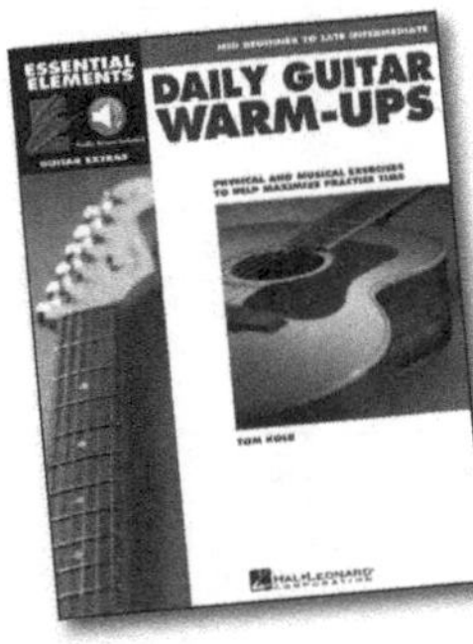

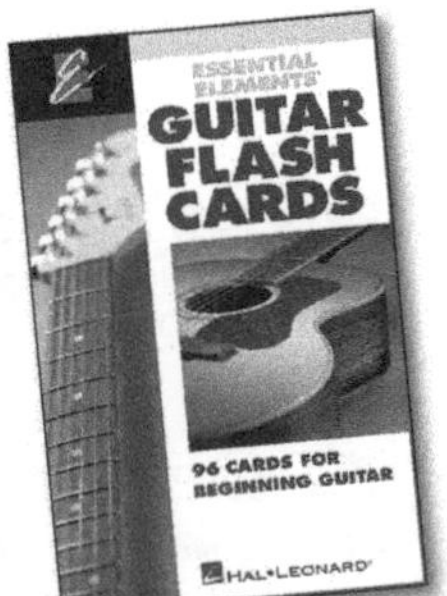

DAILY GUITAR WARM-UPS
by Tom Kolb
Mid-Beginner to Late Intermediate
00865004 Book/Online Audio............................$14.99

GUITAR FLASH CARDS
96 Cards for Beginning Guitar
00865000...$12.99

Prices, contents, and availability subject to change without notice.

HAL•LEONARD®
www.halleonard.com